subversive
sonnets

BOOKS BY PAMELA MORDECAI

POETRY
Journey Poem (1989)
de man: a performance poem (1995)
Certifiable (2001)
The True Blue of Islands (2005)

FICTION
Pink Icing and other stories (2006)

NONFICTION
Culture and Customs of Jamaica (with Martin Mordecai) (2001)

FOR CHILDREN
Storypoems: a First Collection (1987)
Don't Ever Wake a Snake (1992)
Ezra's Goldfish and other storypoems (1993)
The Costume Parade (2000)
The Birthday Party (2000)

subversive
sonnets

poems

PAMELA MORDECAI

We acknowledge the support of the Canada Council for the Arts for our publishing program. We also acknowledge support from the Government of Ontario through the Ontario Arts Council.

We acknowledge the financial support of the Government of Canada through the Canada Book Fund for our publishing activities.

        Canada

Cover design by Ingrid Paulson

Library and Archives Canada Cataloguing in Publication

Mordecai, Pamela
        Subversive sonnets : poems / Pamela Mordecai.

ISBN 978-1-894770-94-1

        I. Title.

PS8576.O6287S82 2012   C811'.54   C2012-905365-1

Printed and bound in Canada by Coach House Printing

TSAR Publications
P. O. Box 6996, Station A
Toronto, Ontario M5W 1X7
Canada

www.tsarbooks.com

For Martin

Contents

Stone Soup

For Irene Armond, trapped under the rubble of the J & B Machado Tobacco Company Factory in the 1907 earthquake in Kingston, Jamaica, who lived to be 101 years of age.

Harker's Hall. Irene and Mama visiting Aunt Clare.
Rene (her nickname) was seven. Alone,
capering in the curious damp cool, she lit
upon a garden with a looping bed of best
ox-heart tomatoes. Green. She ate until,
diligent caterpillar, every plant was bare.
Calling the wages of her greedy sin upon her head,
Mama threatened cramps and colic. She'd be so ill!
Rene let Mama down. She wasn't sick a bit.
"Your stomach strong, girl child!" Cookie told her.
"And if you mind tough like your belly, you
will do!" "Do what, Ma'am?" Staring at Rene,
the woman clapped her hands, showered the child
with flour and said, "You will grow. You will see."

Girls at J & B Machado Tobacco Factory
stop work each day when the korchi blows four.
When Rene looks up the ancient black hands
stretching exhausted on the wall—
they're always fast—show half-past-three,
"Just over half an hour to go . . . " thinking,
as the floor under her rises, buckles,
kicks out like a mad mule. She falls, striking

her head, hearing it crack. Dot's frilly skirt
flares beside her, a crimson flash, just like
the bright stuff on the powdery grey arm
lying across her front. Then nothing, not a thing,
until some ciphers crinkled on a scree of stone,
"*J and B Machado Tobacco.*" But the *Factory's* gone.

She's Cinderella, dead tired, hot as live coals.
The cooked-flesh smell that preachers promise souls
destined for hell seasons gusts from the sea. They sear
her tongue, as dark crumbles to the rare glow
that is dawn's messenger in Potters' Row.
But she can't understand how that can that be.
She was rolling cigars at half-past-three.
And then great ashen wings chastise the sky,
beat down the brightness, banish it to black.
Angels swing brimstone censers as they fly
over, a ghost guard scattering white lime.
Maybe she's died from cholera and it's time
to burn her corpse. She tries to look about
for Dot but her neck swears. Better to use her mouth.

"Dot? Answer me!" Her lips shape only air.
She orders sound. "Dot!" Nothing. "Dotty Blair!"
Fine white flakes blanket her, a kindly squall
stirred by a moth. Cookie from Harker's Hall!
She's grown but stuck here what is she to do?
as every noise in all the world, a stew
of boots' tread, trundled carts, shrieking sirens,

thunder, galloping hooves, grating machines,
explosions cauterize her head and heart.
Flat on her back nailed to her cross of dirt,
she licks her lips and knows how Jesus felt,
beseeching his tormentors for a drop to melt
his clotted thirst. "Come on, girl!" She feels for a stone,
licks it off, puts it underneath her tongue,

where it installs a little pool of spit
between her bottom teeth. She flushes grit
and dirt from round her mouth and like an infant bubbles it
through her closed lips, all the while suckled by her magic rock.
Like an infant she sucks herself to sleep.
Mama is telling the old story of stone soup. "A cheap
and easy dinner to cook up, for each
person gives a gift to the pot." She chuckles. "Teach
a child the way to make this recipe
and nobody they know will go hungry!"
Night wakes her with a choir of little feet
and voices. "This way, sir. We hear her from the street.
We couldn't see her, but we hear her good.
She was laughing and talking about food!"

Old Diaries

Good mustard . . . adds . . . to the palatability of mutton,
bacon, cheese, fish, and even eggs.
                    GRANDPA LOUIS, *Diary and Memorandum Book 1909*

I read his *Diary and Memorandum Book,*
Nineteen O Nine. Printed by De La Rue and Co.,
"With compliments from J & J Colman"—the mustard folks.
The book tells me my light-skinned grandfather
was a small man: hat size six-and-a-half, shoe size
seven, collar size fourteen-and-a-half. I recall him
unsparingly solid and tall. Today I learned he shot a man
for stealing his newspaper. My unforbearing forebear
put a bullet in somebody because the fellow swiped
his daily rag! But I can't fathom this,
hoodwinked by the peacock in Grandpa's yard
throwing back his bejeweled head to bleat "Ow Ow,"
baring his teeth to make thieves likely know
not every thing that's pretty is worthless.

My trigger-happy grandfather had rights
and property. So what is black and white
and read—and all over the nearly dead?
Gramps' newspaper in blasted burglar hands!
No use make joke and lose history's strands
neither forget the heart of man in its
desperate wickedness. Grandpa's grandpa
forty-five years before gave the order

to forces of His Majesty's militia
to open fire on angry slaves storming
the courthouse in Morant Bay. We would like to think
the Baptist minister, Paul Bogle, their leader,
was our relation on our mother's side,
for Bogle was Grandma's born name. It's true

Granny was fair but Mother Africa
had written otherwise all over her:
big lip, big bosom, broad backside. Her privilege
was sew, cook, clean, care sick and mind baby,
boil bush, ignore the law and draw a little ganja tea.
She set her solid self before bad mind and penury
and dared them come. Gran's Diary was her grocery book
that tallied goods she got on trust from Chen
until Gramps got his paycheck come weekend.
My father's father owned a business: thread,
pins, needles, buttons, zips, brought in and spread
like savories through the town. Gran's cottage industry
(a little sewing for money) helped to gobble them down.

Ma's Ma kept laying fowls and eating fowls
in the big chicken coop at Prince of Wales.
Pa's Pa's peacocks at Elletson for show
paraded pouting heads and fanning tails
no mind they might have earned their way.
Those birds watch good as bad dog any day!
Gran used eggs for our daily bread as well
as cookies, cakes and tarts for Chen to sell

up at the shop. (She never let Gramps know.)
On Sundays Granny wrung fowl necks for chow
while every day my Grandpa and his gun
looked out for pilferers who were bent on
thiefing his precious *Daily News*—
a fatal time in want of mustard for tempering stews.

Lace Makers

For Tony McNeill

At the Girls' School black and white nuns
with turned-out toes waddle like penguins on
flippers of buttoned grandma shoes and teach
us to make lace. Us is twelve girls, orphaned,
abandoned or wards of the court. We toss
pegs with round heads, silk cords fitted
inside a notch about each throat, coffles
to yoke brown necks in common service, ours
and theirs. Our warm wood castanets tumble
as lace bubbles like froth, spit threads knitting
to fashion webs of filigree. Gaoled in the shade
of this old lignum vitae tree, we make music,
giggling when we hear Sister Mercedes talk
Jamaican with her funny accent and twist tongue.

Reverend Mother Luke glares at us and declares,
"At seventeen Sister Mercedes waved
goodbye to mother, father, family
as she left home, another island in
a distant sea. And that was thirty years
ago. Ever since she has served young women here
like a born saint. Let me assure you none
of us assumed this call for fun." How anyone
could "mother" that woman upon whose body not

one hair is nurturing confound the likes
of me. Mercedes, now, she know we laugh
at her tie-tongue but she don't mind. She say
after she cross Atlantic and get off
the jitterbugging boat she rock and retch for days.

She never know water could be so wide;
never think she would reach the other side.
And then war come. Her people disappear.
She never hear from them again, know she
cannot go back. "Dis is my home.
De sisters, you, my friends, de people here . . . "
her arms a compass, stretch encompassing,
"all is my family. He take de blood
relations, yes. But see what bounty He
give me?" Her accent sewn into her mouth
like ours, the exact same as when she came.
She and the other two black and white birds
who teach us how to use these sticks enjoy our raw-
chaw dialect. They try it out. "Owdy! Unoo earty?"

Meanwhile Mother Luke leans hard on the horn
of her red Ford—first woman in this whole
island to drive a conveyance not pulled
by four-footed creatures. Her long black skirt
slung in between her knees, beads furled into
her lap, dark glasses on her white bent nose,
she drive rough as any crufty truck man.
She deal out punishment—called "just desserts"—

in the same way. One day she and me catch
a fight over the strap she use to give us licks.
All now they tell the tale of how I wrench
it from her hand, fling it clear through
the window and proclaim, "White lady, me
not fraid of you. Is you should shame! How you

could say you working in God's name while you
murder us with this strap?" You want see jawbone drop
that day! That time Mercedes raise her voice,
"Luke, why you beat the child? Look how long I
been telling you beating don't do no good?"
That sweet Mercedes come and find me up at my
grandmother's ground. She tell Gran, "Rosie make
lace like she learn it in the womb." When I reach here
and find the fashion district on Queen Street,
I make lace and save my money till I buy my own
boutique. Claude McKay say he remember
poinsettias in December. I recall red blooms as well:
three old nuns, faces flushed and wrinkled up as mace,
under a tree conjuring waves of foaming Maltese lace.

Family Story: Only Child's Version

My father fair with his straight nose and hair
kept chickens and a goat. No country backra, city wise
farming for him a sheer subsistence enterprise.
He built boats too, and houses, furniture
with those fair hands. Never kiss ass, owe penny, shirk,
give for a day's pay less than a day's work,
carry down any boss-man even one day of his life.
As for my Ma, his soulful coolie wife,
she was a slow-eyed, deep, dark teacher girl,
too sensitive for this dog-eat-cat world,
her body slim and sad after it kicked
out infants, one, then two, then three,
who each in dashed hope burgeoned her belly,
until, God help her, it delivered me.

I was too much for Ma. I made her walk
and jabber to herself. Hopeless and helpless she'd
take to the street, clothes in a paper bag
or handkerchief tied to a stick, headed
for where beneath some car, some bridge or down
some precipice, she hoped she'd find relief.
Futile, for it ran in the family.
Her father walked just so into the sea
one day, leaving Grandma with twelve crosses.
(He'd lost his job but no one knew.) What could
Gran do? Wash, iron, cook, and mind the neighbor kids.

Better than Gramps, for jobs for men were criminal
or none. Small wonder he chucked himself in.
Humiliated, Grandpa cut his losses.

Which leaves—guess who? Madness you understand
breeds like the Black Death, hooks your DNA,
combines and recombines, nests, starts a brood.
Hijacked you find yourself enmeshed in
accidental love affairs: with bed, which of
a sudden you must cling to and cannot desert.
To rise is faithless. It's the opposite with dirt.
Dirt is infatuated, stalks you, will not let
you be. Small crawly things journey
across your scalp, wriggle under your arms, reside
inside your ears, between your toes. They drill
into your teeth, they eat your nose. You wash,
you clean, you scrub, you floss to no avail.
Things thrive under each toe and fingernail.

And so you yield, give in, give up the ghost.
Too tired to fight it, turn a willing host.
You do not bathe. The little guests, welcome,
survive and breed. And now the voices you
have warded off come in, a great cacophony,
a holy din. Imagine Gramps waking to this
each day: to twelve offspring, a fertile wife,
all the dismay of love and feed and nurture and
provide, the cliché's roe unhoe-able, the horse
too wild to ride. Imagine Ma chased by

these demons, tending to no child but a
fierce, tortured, yelping thing. These mutants are
our lives, Gramps', Mama's, mine, wraiths that we see.
But I'm here. Careful then how you cross me.

On Friendship Avenue

For EAW

I will cling to the old rugged cross,
And exchange it some day for a crown.
                    (A popular hymn)

We walk down Friendship Avenue to get the bus,
me on one side, then Rich, then Lillibet.
Rich holds on tight to us for every day
Ma chronicles the perils that await
impetuous pedestrians. I who hate grimy trek,
bus, school, look down and try to hypnotize
my stubborn feet. "Rose, why you always walk
with your head down? After God give you that
nice nose! Don't make bad duppy fool you, when
you dead, that head going drop down by itself.
Better hold it up now!" I love Aunt C, so if
she say, then I obey. Brown faces hoisted to the sun,
we tramp through marly dust inscribed by tracks
of trucks with crab-toe squiggles like our copybooks.

We pass the Holiness Deliverance Tent
whose Reverend Capleton reminds us evenings on
his megaphone that if we don't accept
Jesus Christ as our Personal Saviour
and get on board his soon-to-leave salvation train,
we will be damned. A hiss at the bus stop . . .

Chi-cheee. We scramble up as doors close on
penny-ha'penny hostages, confine
them in a steaming hold. With every jolt,
sweating foreheads, cheeks, arms and legs collide
with flapping body parts. Lillibet hugs
Rich on her lap. On a bad turn he slams
his lip into the rail in front. He wails
but not enough for all the children on the bus.

Sunday. Our tireless tricycle turns on
its rind of cork as we eddy around a clump
of crown-of-thorns. I hold on from behind.
Lillibet churns the wheels yelling, "Don't strangle me!"
Come six o'clock "Old rugged cross" grieves from
a tent packed till the saints in scalding white,
cherubim squalling round their feet, brim over, spill
into the street. So what if they lift up
a soulful noise unto the Lord? God knows His One
True Catholic Church and they're not it, so they can cling
till their fists twist, and sing till their misguided lungs
give out—or till the tent collapse. And it would serve
them right . . . whose songs have served me well,
redemption more than any reverend's promise of hell.

Nutrament

Papa comes home for lunch: two sandwiches—
brown bread, lettuce, slice of tomato, wisp of cheese.
Us children get one each. "Chew thirty-two times!" Auntie C
swivels her mandibles. "That way you get
the nutrament inside the food." We giggle for
we know the difference. *Nutrament* is what
the fat lady next door drinks every time before
she eats a huge dinner. She says she's dieting.
We like the cool of Mama's grapefruit juice
sweetened with brown sugar and mixed with ginger ale,
choking with ice. Two bottles can stretch two
grapefruits for five of us. Richard,
the smallest, says grace-before-meals. After
we eat Papa intones, "Laus tibi, Christi, domine!"

He likes to pray in Latin. It lifts him
above his neighbor to a godly plain
reserved for those who speak strange languages.
Auntie Cleo teases him with the tongue
she got when the Holy Spirit infiltrated her.
"Don't bring none of that obeah in this house!"
Papa warns. She will croon in Aramaic though
(so she says), if we beg her hard. "If you
are ever in a room of folks singing
in tongues, you'll hear how heavenly choirs sound!"
Our eyes pop out. Nobody that we know

has heard the angels raise a tune. Papa stays after lunch
just for a bit. He does the crossword (quick
and then cryptic) in his armchair made by

his hand, mahogany seasoned by sweat
and wear and not no store-bought piece
of furniture. Upholstered seat and back
and padding on the arms are nods to comfort. "For
when you get old," Auntie cackles like a mad hen
if you push her from off her nest of eggs,
"you also get a bony ass!" "Cleo!"
Ma makes like she is vex. "Why you must talk
like that before the children-them?" Auntie
kisses her teeth and swings her large rear end
like she's a hula doll. Papa don't deign
to notice them, inks a word, then another, settles back,
puts the newspaper on his face, applies himself
so fervently to sleep his snores swoop out the gate.

Cleo believes that all things move and have
their being in God who is shaped like an egg.
 "You know the earth goes round the sun?" We nod.
"And turns around itself?" We nod again.
Her eyes prance between Lillibet and me
like a small dog showing off a new bone.
"Well the whole universe revolves like that.
And God show us some of its mysteries."
She tears newspaper, shows us how to make
a Moebius strip. "If anybody tells you there's

no God, just show them this." For five decades I've hung
onto that one-side piece of paper, bangle of
eternity, that Cleo cut for us that afternoon
pasting its ends together with her spit.

Introibo ad altare dei

Pops nibbled Latin through the English mass
determined the demotic should not pass
his ritual ears. Glum brood in tow, he went religiously
every Sunday. When force-ripe progeny
refused to go, he made do with the willing few.
We never saw him take communion though,
which meant our virtuous Pops was always in—
Ora pro nobis, Maria—a state of serious sin!
For sure our whole life long we never saw
Pops slip behind the drape into the maw
of the confessional, a dreadful place,
hardly forgiving, more a sinning space.
Who could blame Pops? Who would elect to go
into that cell, head bucking to and fro,

rat trapped in medieval dark until the grate
slid by to show a pink expatriate pate
sweating a pale blue foreign eye? Well not
our Pops. As for us foolish female lot,
hog-tied by a dominant narrative,
an object lesson in comparative
discomfort, taught by nuns, those subtle saints,
serpentine, insisting that once the taints
of sin had been removed—ego te absolvo—
the joy, the sense of freedom we would know,
the ordeal done, the curtain cast aside,

our laundered soul now turned a worthy bride
for the deathless bridegroom our sweet Lord—
why it was worth each coughed-up, wrenched-out word,

each patwa worm turned wriggling from the muck
of our disgusting lives! Of course with just a little luck
we would have figured homo sapiens are male,
and it is they who shrive; women female,
and to be shriven. Concerning sin, God had
an understanding with the gender he first made.
So we were meant to cower in the dark
but Pops was not. It would become a stark
reminder of the substance of our being
our calling to be led, eyes closed, unseeing,
chanting in some strange tongue what some man said—
the pope, the priest—some servile of our sex relayed.
Surely you who loved women, you, Oh Lord,
sold like a slave, sentenced upon the word

of clerics who swore in lofty Hebrew
that for fomenting insurrection you,
speaker of Aramaic, a gutter tongue,
should be serrated, seasoned, peppered, slung
upon a spit, not all that gore so fakes
mouthing Rome's standard dialect,
selling blessings and pardons, might effect
a new imperium proscribing us? Dying, around your feet
pierced, weeping red, your winding sheet

ready to hand, you saw your mother with women
who gave the lie to our sex as fearful, flimsy dames.
Remember, never mind your Good Book blames
Eve for our dicey situation, absent Mary's vulgar Amen
joining your Father's bet, there'd be no incarnation.

No problema, Doc

Doc's a nice man. Each time he probes, Are you thinking
of hurting somebody? Harming yourself?
You can't mean there are folks who tell you yes?
I ask. You'd be surprised, says he. I tell him I
would be. This morning I get out of bed,
get in the shower (first for days),
stand dripping wet before the mirror, check
my lipstick "To do" list. 1. Therapist.
2. Pry more money out of bank. 3. Legal aid.
4. Bury the damn cat. Through the red scrawl
I see contours on a dry yellow map,
kouris for streams, valleys for rivers in
full flood. I know the landscape well. I breathe
into my palms—and smell ripe jungle mouth.

Lioness must have slept last night after she dined
on rotten pig! Or put the native way
my cakehole, also known as pie-hole, stinks.
(Not one person I know in the real world
speaks of a mouth in pastry terms!) But to
the matter of the morning's moment: needs
must open said foul mouth to speak to shrink,
so halitosis will not do. I scour my tongue
with my toothbrush and sniff again. Still gross.
What now? Salt in hot water; if that fails
to work, lime juice. I hunt clean jeans and find

a pair. Impale a shoe then spear its twin.
You going down to the doc in your brassiere?
That is my spouse, comic at large. I haul a shirt

on, check for dirt under my nails, the one or two
I've not chewed to green dots, clap a cool cap
on my hot head to hide the disarray.
En route I'll daub some powder and a bit
of gloss. Et voilà! Hello, Dr J. Not bad,
thanks. How are you? True, things are better now
it's spring. I do. I take my meds though some-
times I forget and then I take too many then
too few. I know I shouldn't but what can
I do if I forget? And as you say,
clinically there's nothing wrong with me.
I'm not going to OD, jump off a high
rise, set the neighbour's house on fire. You know
me. No problema, Doc. When I do harm, it's harmlessly.

This Is the Way

Monday. This is the way we wash our clothes.
Whites on this side for they need special care.
Put the darks yonder in a separate pile.
Sort coloureds—light, not-so-light, darkish over here,
each shade in its right place as the hymn says.
Whites in the water first as it behooves,
gentled in Ivory flakes with temperate scrub,
then set on coral stones to profit from the sun's
abundant coin. Now and then, on tougher stains, rub
with brown soap and a tip of Adam's ale
till blemishes erased, garments gleam clean.
Coloureds get shrift according as they pale.
Darks last, slapped on the beating stone, hung on the fence.
To coddle drubbing clothes don't make no sense.

Tuesday. This is the way we iron our clothes.
Whites first again, sweated clean on the bleach,
blued, starched, rinsed, pegged to the high wire,
hoisted by sturdy line-sticks, so no mess contrived
by beasts marauding in the dirt below
smudge their refurbished purity.
Perverse, we sprinkle them after we pluck
them dry, foreplay that readies them to mate
with macho irons that await
on phosphorescent coals. Unfurl them in
damp turn, sweating, breath bated, for

that sumptuous, countering hiss. Brush off
the irons' dark bodies. Touch them down.
Satisfy with a long slow-burning kiss.

Wednesday. This is the day we conjure clothes.
The bill collector comes to our home
the day I fashion my first frock, costume
threaded like damask with a honeycomb
of flowers in blue black, seed pods, trellises
of dark green leaves. I'm all of eight as I deduce
how to employ Grandma's machine, no juice
to move it and no treadle for my feet to pump;
instead a wheel my hands must turn. "If need
be," Gran assures, "needle and thread alone
can make a seam with back or running stitch!"
As babes we jumped at sorties to Miss Ida on Glenmore
to fit us with frilly confections. Now, basted,
hemmed, cobbled by ourselves, we flaunt our *bas couture*.

Thursday. This is the way we mend our clothes
or did one time for it seems not a soul
wants patching up these days. Raiment
that's torn, unraveled, frayed, distressed
is best disposed of, so the experts warn.
According to them, judged objectively,
all things considered, it's sage policy,
the lightest footprint. No need to give a darn.
"Why waste time fixing it? Go buy one new."
No vintage threads. No retro in their view.

We don't redeem, repair, restore. We toss the dregs.
My mother had three wooden darning eggs,
her mama, a moody mending machine. I try
to salvage cast-offs with a frenzied eye.

Friday. This is the day for drudging wear.
Dawn scrapes light from the dark as we unearth
yam, tania, arrowroot, shoveling clouds
gray as our desperation in grim piles
that turn up tubers shriveled as our skins.
Outfits for field and forage, tattered gear
rend as we do for night will find us hard
done by. Fingers scurry to scrub off prickling dirt,
load bag on bag to warm a bruckdown bus
with a blanket of baskets, broody mound
of bankra eyes that stare us down to town
to market where we keen, "Look miss! Here chief!
Come. Stretch your money. One dollar a pound
for dasheen, irish, cassava . . . " rending also our hearts.

Saturday. The day that we inventory
the meagre store of coverings for our backs—
shirts, trousers, jackets, shorts, skirts, blouses, frocks,
slips, nighties, singlets, sweaters, stockings, socks,
pajamas—each shrinking thing handed on,
every item a guarded legacy.
So blue subsides to eggshell, red to rose
to pink. Black dims to ashen, then pale gray.
We wear them thin. This is the way

we stretch nothing so something comes of it.
Whoever said, "Ex nihilo nihil fit" had
not a notion of what nothing is worth.
We glean in ruin, passing on what's left.
Only the gods can truly scorch the earth.

Sunday. The day a body should sleep late,
eat a good country breakfast, a full plate,
codfish and ackee or mackerel run-down.
But no. This is the day we don our best,
fighting up with a long-sleeve high-neck dress,
a shirt so stiff its collar stands to gloat
and execute a sentence on our throat.
We trudge to church, weary feet mashing green,
some come for worship, some just to be seen,
splendid arrivants, garments bright as snow—
tomorrow's drudgery. Pews a rainbow
of colours, light to dark, pray that we mend
and throw mites, trusting that because we spend,
husbanding nought, and meek, we'll buy another week.

Reading at 4:00 AM

1 Reading the Poets

i

I read Walcott's *Omeros*, chapter six. Helen
chats with her friends down near to the sea wall.
She don't like when the tourist foreigners
put their hands on her ass and so she tell
the cashier he could keep the fucking job.
Is just a stupid waitress work, is all!
Only she now must find something to do
like how she pregnant and don't know for who.
For me her tale is poetry more than
"love songs fading over a firefly sea."
(chapter eleven). If ocean, hill and sky
can't hold this odyssey, what chance a page?
I set aside the book to search my face
for prudent lines to whisper to Helen.

ii

I read a poem, "Mint," about a tuft
of fine-leaved crimp-edged aromatic stalks
in Seamus Heaney's yard—we had one too
on the way down the slope to the back gate.
Nobody planted it; it was just there
from the beginning, so for all I know
it's maybe standing still, its slender waist

not a whit bigger, growing its spicy grow.
It's a fine poem. I see what Heaney says
and magic don't come much in verse these days
except in songs from worlds where minstrels tune
their notes for bread because, don't mind how much
rain fall, the dirt, like Miss Lou says, is tough,
and nothing grows to feed our souls enough.

iii
I read Larkin's "This Be the Verse." Tough poem.
It says your parents fuck you up. They do.
It says that they don't mean to. I'm less sure
that absence of malevolence is true
in every case. It says that they were fucked
up in their turn by parents who wore old-
style hats and coats, outfits I'm sure that made
them neither less nor more effective passers-on
of grief! It says, "Man hands on misery
to man . . . " Present enough, but no, this passing on
"it deepens like a coastal shelf." (Perhaps
we'd best look up our topographic terms?)
To sound the image and the ocean floor
requires resonance. The same thing holds for agony.

iv

The day you left the air broke
into splinters

DIONNE BRAND, *Inventory,* p. 61

If you think you're indispensable, consider,
when you pull out your fist, what happens to water.
(A saying)

I read *Inventory,* page sixty-one. A fist
won't make an empty space in water when
the hand immersed comes out unless
that hand belongs to someone quick enough
to break the air in shards: the elements
are subject then. Marlene's in blue in a new house
on her birthday. That time I read at Harbourfront,
she sent to say, "I'm sorry that I'm sick.
I would have loved to hear you read." I told
her, "Anytime you wish, just send to tell
me and I'll bring my poems and come." We read
for her that last birthday, my poet friend and me.
Now she prophetic with a pen parts water on
page sixty-one to show the space a fist can make.

II Reading The World Wide Web

i

I read that animals can't fool themselves.
They know when they have fouled their habitats.

They know inside their breasts and blood and wings—
all animals that is but human beings.
It's only us, the smartest of the lot,
who sit inside this slowly heating pot
like frogs saying the temperature's the same.
Spring chickens spinning in a stewing sludge,
we sit and peck our corn and do not budge,
we wriggle in our excrement and crow
our disavowal choosing not to know.
Ah, Pope, I've stole your pen and plainly spoke,
which they like not, in rhythm and in rhyme
so they'll not hearken—till there's no more time.

ii

I read at night I should make sure it's deep
and darkest black in places where I sleep.
That way my cells can conjure melanin.
It darkens skin and spares us from disease,
those malefactoring metastases.
Of course chance is, however dim the shades,
cancer going get me; for sure I going dead.
Can't put my head to that, Lord, for just now
the taxman cometh, him to whom I bow,
doing obey/i/sans a foot to stand on,
if I treat these tax forms with the abandon
I judge them to deserve. So rich
and righteous get their just desserts—
the poor as ever sigh and lift their skirts.

iii

I read one day Alpha and Omega
took it in mind to scrape a ball of clay
and cough into the clod. Whereupon sprouted it
two feet and branched it blood and bloomed it brain
and standing over all proclaimed dominion.
Eden it was, in Ethiopia. First it
was good, then not so good. But stayed they still
until another day, tired perhaps
to brawl for food or bored or stricken by
disease, skin blistering like bubbles in the surf,
or baited by a hunch of better fish to fry,
a ragged band set off toward a sea as distant as
old age. Foot over foot through sand,
by Bab-el-Mandeb and the Persian Gulf to India,

a far, far ways to travel, yes . . . And then by one
almighty walkabout across the isles
of Andaman and Nicobar through Melanesia,
their offspring reached, perhaps making
landfall within the glow of Bungle Bungle, a
fat land that Master Hakluyt later called
Australia. Forty-five thousand years
ago we came, well before other Aethiop kin
trekked north, grew cold as ice, bit their lips thin,
lost their hair's curl, turned colourless as snow—
European. So bredren we is dem
and dem is we, cousin and cousin clearly darkly knit

by slavish habits, bone, psoriasis and sweat,
doubt, dereliction and the fear of debt.

Cockpit Country*—A Tasting Tour

Mapping the fjords between my fingers, you
make shore in the soft shallow of my palm.
You rest there, savoring the score, the notes
that gypsies say are the book for my life.
It is an easy journey, my forearm, but thirsty, you
linger to lick sweat in my elbow, then
climbing the smooth slope of my upper arm,
you gain my shoulder, pause like a small cat
curling to catch a nap. You wake, surveying the
terrain and see limber before you, mound
on mound of cockpit country, breasts, belly
and thighs, and round beyond the swell of hips
but well in reach, plump cheeks, a booty worth
the find. You go ahead, because it's what
you do, adventurer, no mind that sinkholes lurk

to trap the best spelunkers, for they say
numberless men have lost themselves inside
such secret caves, their ink black waters still
as death. You'll vanish inside neither nook
nor cave, anchored firm as you are. Where you

*Cockpit country is a roughly 500-square-mile (1,300-square-
kilometre) region in the interior of Jamaica, southeast of Montego Bay.
It is part of the great White Limestone plateau and has typical karst
topography, with numerous conical and hemispherical hills covered
with dense scrubby trees, rising hundreds of feet over depressions and
sinkholes with sharp, precipitous sides.

reside, breezes blow warm, regular, stopped
only in awe, in ecstasy, when something takes
your very breath away. And so, you have no fear,
sinuous wriggler, you journey on, careless
that after you and jealous in your wake,
comes the diviner, lightning rod, great one
who conjures rain. But even if he's many times
your size, and dark, and thick, theatrical,
terrible, thunder-bearing, you know well

his staying power can't match yours.
He'll loom large, wind the wind up, crash about,
arrange some fireworks, blow up a storm,
send shivers down a poor girl's spine; but when
he's done, he's done, while you are in the pink,
ready like a good scout at any time
of day or night for charting landscape, yes,
but that done, after love, for life as well,
sweet worm who's lapped up tears, pulled mucus from
occluded passages, cleaned wounds, sucked breasts
to draw down milk and balled up food for tiny throats.
And with this, all along, interpreted
the songs written across this wrinkling skin
and sung them, every day, lively and long and lingering.

Counting the Ways and Marrying True Minds

How do I love thee? Let me count the Ways.
Way One is forty on his next birthday.
Way Two is pregnant with our first grandchild;
at thirty-eight she's finding her first way
to loving her own man. Way Three? Way Three,
Wash-Belly, is the last one to abide,
for when, according to my OBG,
you set them sweetly in my sweet inside,
for each Way hanging on, there was a Way
that saw the world outside and would not stay.
So Way Three, manic, mad, magnificent,
speaks the last lines in this soliloquy
of how your cells have swelled inside my cells,
of how your flesh has truly become me.

Will may be jealous for the marriage of true minds
but what's the harm in an impediment
or two? I think of Auntie Vida with her tale
about her bawdy bad-behaving friend
telling a lover who protested he
and she were incompatible, "Oh no,
my dear! You're not looking at this in the
right way at all." Shoulders thrown back to elevate
her beauties in their bloom, she set him straight,
"You have the income. I am pattable."
Mind's not the only measure, only mate,
and love obstructed may revise itself and change,

and change again, and with each alteration, grow.
Fixed marks make easy targets. So our love

has bobbed and weaved to pass the edge of doom.
No mates in heaven yet we have a pact.
You've promised you will not ignore me who
have loved you many ways. I, beyond strife,
will once and finally be still, touching
no mouse, keyboard, nor pen, nor quill,
no fork nor spade, hammer nor nail, nor broom,
vacuum, mop, nor pail, touching only
on God and his fine Son, consummate bride-
groom, and on Wisdom, she through whom I lit
on you, sweet other one in whom I found
three perfect Ways to love. So let it be.
Awash in honeyed obstacles, you'll make
a keen addition to the choir. I'll be around.

Temitope

temitope: Yoruba, "enough to give thanks" or "give thanks to God."
A name for both males and females, though more often females.
igba: Many meanings including "rope," "two hundred," "time/season,"
"garden egg."
Olorun: Creator, Supreme Being, one of many names for the Yoruba
Sky God.

My daughter tells me, "Mum, I don't have much
more time, so I do not intend to read
hundreds of baby books." She's thirty-eight.
The girl child she is carrying is her first.
I tell her, "Love, it isn't very kind
of you to tell someone who's sixty-four
about not having much more time!"
But it is really fine. We say it is
longer than rope, this time, this word that has
no synonym, being itself or not
itself, being, rather, liminal, an interstice
between just then and a moment about
to be. But we who come from islands know,
crac-cric, periphrastic, is so life go.

And as for baby books, we never read
not one. We birthed you, named you, kept you clean,
fed you, sent you to school, prayed God you would
come to no harm. That cord of hours played out
by tiefing hands so long ago to snare you on your way

back home, waterjar on your head, humming
as your swift feet spat sand, slant eyes smiled at
the spinning wheel of huts ahead, ears shut
against the loud demanding threads of smoke
from their cook fires, "Sapling, how come we wait
the whole day and you don't reach home?" And then,
"How come you fade like mist and nobody see you again?"
How could we know a coffle choked your song
air buckled in your throat as you grew thin

down a rats' hole dug deep in watery dirt?
How could we know they flayed your bark with whips
rammed you between felled trees trussed end to end
seasoned in vomit, blood and shit? Our tears
spilled from closed eyes scoured pots of memory
as fitful slumber tossed our heads, tumbled our dreams.
We sought to conjure labyrinths crisscrossed
by footprints shouting still, "Time you reach home!"
We counted cowries hours, weeks, centuries.
We prayed, day-clean and dark, "Olorun grant
the stolen ones igba, a rope to climb
out of fate's pit to eat sweet dates again,
to see through green lashes of leaves your home of sky."
Olorun heard. The infant came on a red string. Temitope.

Zoey Stands Up to Schrodinger's Cat

Life is cheap and death still cheaper,
where the sun only is their keeper.

(A saying)

She says, "Zoey stand up!" then "Zoey tall!"
and so she is upon a kitchen chair
a splendid coruscation at age two.
I'm Grandma grappling with Schrodinger's Cat.
It's hard because I'm haunted in the way
old age engages blood and bones and brain
in every little business of its life
with the bizarre idea we do not need
the gentleman, his here-now, there-now cat,
neither dark matter, chaos theory, memes,
the selfish gene, nor quantum mechanics
ever at odds with relativity, no mind
the latter is succinctly put: $E=MC^2$.
I put aside the putative feline

for my Zoey grandchild, her atoms volatile
as her impulse to take a flying leap
from off the chair. She is about to be
older, bolder, Icarus' progeny
testing out space. "Catch me, Dada!" She's here
and she's   elsewhere. But then it's no great feat
to be in two places at once, not for

inveterate immigrants who have seen
contrary things the same in history's way,
our language and our lives. We watch the Zoe
as swift, celestial and dimensionless
she takes to air, rowdy as any sprite
inebriated and astray in nutmeg groves,
and falls upon the cat. It howls like it's in heat

and I see why Schrodinger didn't choose to use
that staple of experiment, *mus musculus,*
the common household mouse. I jest of course.
It is a test in mind and not in fact.
If scientific curiosity coldly deprives (perhaps)
the poor cat of its life, it hardly matters since
the cat must have existences to spare
in its imagined state as well. In which
respect, cat is like us who're suckled by the sun,
of whom it's said, however life is cheap,
death is an even less costly alternative.
Therefore for all the world like the atomic cat
we're dead alive. But Zoey knows it is
as in dead centre, drop-dead fabulous.

From Everlasting to Everlasting

For JJ

> The corn was orient and immortal wheat, which never should be
> reaped, nor was ever sown. I thought it had stood from everlasting
> to everlasting.
>
> THOMAS TRAHERNE, *Centuries of Meditations*

After our week of prayer, friend, we tried
to say goodbye to you, our spirit guide.
They said you'd gone off in the blue VW with Lee, a tall
archangel with a limp. I don't recall
who else was in our group—just you, Martin,
Lee, Sister Miriam, and me. Lee had flown in
from Maine. Us other four, two bredren, two sistren,
had worked one time in Jamdown, land of water
and wood, paradise island that like all
utopias and children's games boasted a fall.
Not born-there, Sister Miriam and you, John,
had set down, toiled like worry ants, and gone.
We had left tropic bliss for north and cold,
rats jumping ship, dumping our perfect world.

The mystic Tom Traherne said corn
was orient and immortal wheat, not sown,
not ever to be reaped. His was an esoteric point of view
distracting for apprentice poets who
judged our lands rife with sin, all their sweet rage

a poison succulent from Adam's age,
who saw Eden pristine and its forfeit,
a tale of islands not so full of shit
as it might seem. Hauled here, we supped ruin
with our wicked stepmother's milk. For fun
we learned the ways of sugar, whip and gun:
to grin and kill. Now in the dark, steps we hear bring
us bread or death. So who, poet or sage, proves right?
Fallen it was my blessed chance to light

on you, apple of heaven's eye. Now you have fled
how can I cope with dreams that catapult me from my bed
and send the neighbours scurrying to call the fuzz?
Your ear is not a keypad's dance, a cellie's buzz
away. Not any more. We won't ever agree
again that coming last beats coming two or three
behind the first. I miss your ordinary face.
I miss your hand dismissing sin. I miss the grace
of your big-belly laugh, the filling of the wafer food
become the Son by your magician's word,
broke that we might be sane. So how my friend
could you grind gears, take off sudden,
set for Elijah's fields in that punch buggy car,
and you well know VWs won't take you up that far!

Our Lady of Good Voyage, Gloucester-on-Sea

Our Lady of Good Voyage guards the lives
of all tars exiting this port. They say each day
she's kept that faith, watching the swells (and swells
there are—some homes on Niles Pond Road could hold
a town!) since eighteen ninety-three. Tell that
to Frank, Dale, Alfred Pierre, Robert, Bugsy,
and Dave, crew of the *Andrea Gail,* drowned in
that perfect storm, Mongrel sired by Cyclone out
of Hurricane, in nineteen ninety-one.
Tell Alfie Brown, poor dreamer, the lone sailor lost
the night the Cunard boat, *Roxania,* ran through
the *Mary P* and, cleaving her in two, sent Alf the cook
to join that other fellow with a fork—Neptune,
I mean, though not a doubt the Devil had his fork out too.

There's times it seems to me life's all about
consumption and regurgitation and
more swallowing. Think of Lewis Galdy,
devoured by land, ejected by the sea
in the great quake of sixteen ninety-two
that sent Port Royal, the new world's Sodom,
to watery doom; Jonah, devoured, then coughed
up by the whale; the Mariner in Kipling's tale,
a shipwrecked man "of great sagacity,"
who having been ingested, jumped about
inside leviathan until the monster spat him out!

We're brought here splashing in a womb
that shoves us out, having enticed us in. Meanwhile, a tomb
yawns wide waiting. What sense in all this coming and going?

I ponder this under the Virgin's gaze,
sombered by waves. What if they flood this place
on Mary's watch, sending us soaked to Sheol?
God's Ma upon a breezy slope, dark eyes cutting it up
with funky gulls, as frail craft overturn, cutters
capsize, tempests toss us to gusty kingdom come?
"No one survived," the news will state. "Some in
the Virgin's chapel on their knees recited rosaries. Some bent
before the Sacrament. Some ogled furry odalisques
upon the rocks." Maybe they'll write our names in church
with the drowned dead. Perhaps the history books will say,
"We can learn from their skeletons, as with Pompeii,
what life was like for votives of this cult!"
At least we would have prayed and died believing the result.

But what of Mary, Mother of the Blessed Sea Trip,
who rescues some and throws some back like fish
that will not fetch a decent price? How to
discover when she's up to interceding with
her Son and his Almighty Pa on our behalf?
Or is it that she asks but they just laugh,
whimsical deities who choose by tossing dice?
But willful is as willful does, and after all, we do it,
so why shouldn't they? We are disposed

to murder, state approved or on the side,
contract, freelance or in a hissy fit.
We kill our children with and for a grain of rice.
Who can fuss if from up on high Our Lady Blue
says, "Loves, we do our best. The trouble is with you."

Cozumel*, Island of Swallows

Cuzam: Mayan, "swallow"

In Cozumel, Island of Swallows, tired
iguana lizards droop on dried-out trees,
buff and burnt orange twists of citrus peel
festooned on knotty branches hoping time
will bring this dreary sentence to an end.
Their three eyes scour unblinking our two,
as we click phones and snap them shuffling stairs
where pilgrims gathered once. "Man things," Guido
dismisses them. "This is a woman place.
From all part of this world the women came
to pray to goddess Ixchel for babies
to full their bellies and to beg good medicine—
and rain." As we set sail, clear skies bent by
a rainbow bless the island with his afterthought.

Quintana Roo. The girl who's cadged a ride,
small sister at her side, is red as blood. Perhaps
they scrape them raw with loofahs from the vines
along the shore and leave them tethered there

*Women from through out Mesoamerica traveled to Cozumel to
worship at the shrine of Ixchel ("She of the Rainbow"), Mayan
goddess of childbirth and medicine, fertility and rain. In ancient
times, every Mayan woman was expected, at least once in her
lifetime, to make the journey to Cozumel from the mainland to
make offerings to Ixchel for her family's fertility and for crop
sustenance.

to burn who sin. "Pobrecita!" our driver sighs.
"In the midnight her papa tell her choose
between a hard thing here . . ." he pokes his heart
"or here . . ." patting his crotch. His tale whispers
down through the bus. "Sólo tenía diez!" He lets
the wheel go, lifts ten fingers up. Guido stares dead
ahead. We let her down, dollars shoved at her fierce
dark-eyed Cuzam, then rush through limestone rocks
with cactus stars to find a forest of
earth mounds. "Behold!" swells Guido. "Roads and squares.

Great palaces! A marketplace!" He beams.
"We have unearthed intact a temple tomb untouched
for centuries." I allow his redundancy,
resist the urge to say human things must
be touched. "This other pyramid has been
polluted by continuous use . . . " he shakes
his head, "for everyday affairs: cookhouse,
saloon, small vendor's shack. Such a pity!"
We climb the tainted monument, ankles
turned out, look dizzy down thin steps, offer
an hour's drunken worship bumping down
on our backsides. Below a bird wakes on a branch
erupting through new leaves to plunge into
an ebbing sky. Once more out of the blue it rains.

Zambesi Paean 1995

mhembwe: Shona, "duiker" (small antelope)
Mwari: "supreme god"
vanhu: "people"

Our old imported craft (Ah! but it knows
how to get through) insinuates its way
through driftwood logs, their goggle eyes
(such legerdemain!) closed, yes, but still
waiting on time. Laden it ploughs past sleek-
skinned hippopotami who fan their fat
backsides claiming rights on this Grand River.
A snout submits a yellow yawn methodical
and wide. "Why what sharp teeth you have!" A wit's
observation. Nervy chuckles invade
luxuriant gallery forest green.
Everywhere else in this enormous stone
house, Mwari's land, is thirsty, dry as bone.
Mhembwe perish in droves. Vanhu, old and

young, die as well, but sovereign states
are sovereign and the price extorted by
an evil oligarch is fealty
or death. We reach and tie up at the dock
to rubberneck. There's nothing here but there
is everything. Leaves leap about the sky
strung by their tails. Moulting streams soar and flap
into the bush. Lianas dart tough tongues

to rope the heavens in, lasso the clouds.
The trapped sky belches, hawks, but not a spit
of rain. On the bank frantic apes with eyes
perfect as wounds polished by worms extend
imploring arms in baleful port de bras,
twirl wobbly pirouettes, leap for leftovers flung

at water that laps still as before time.
"Once," says the guide, "we all swam here, reptiles
and all. But now they take what falls in as
fair game." He smiles. We fail to grasp his wry
significance. The vessel turns downstream
towards torrents named after the tubby queen
pouring imperial gallons down a monumental scarp.
Headlong in the slim gorge next door
manic sauteurs bungee jump in
to plunder air—all that's still left.
Trippers disgorging hurl bile on the waves.
Gigantic haunches shrug the vomit off
as sacred crocodiles in camouflage
submerge, and falcons keep watch in the sky.

À l'Ouest Sauvage

For AS and CD

ayisiniwok: Cree, "true men"
iyiniwok: "people"

She swings the corner from Memorial
to Tenth and meets a fierce fiery eye.
Step on your brakes! As if bright green had not
unequivocally declared just now
(others there were to witness it) "Draw the
gears girlie! Get a move on! Go!" The lights
it seems in stampede country can't agree.
She parks, hops out in snow and sees all round
a smooth thin white veneer that hardly hides
set jaws of ice. Circumspect, she leans down
adjusting her centre of gravity
(she's no girl now), watching her step, wary,
each moccasin set just so, left, right, left,
securing her advance for if she slips

a whole concatenation falls with her.
Winds shift fast here. Temperatures change.
The weather is a minute's work. Fate like
the mercury plunges by swift degrees,
freezing maneuvers to secure this space
where true men, ayisiniwok, our kin
planted corn, grew and cured the sacred leaf,

rode their own feet to follow bison flocks,
and after Carbanero's horses came,
joined our bodies to theirs flying
in their fleet hooves. Habitats change.
Strange farmers take on greasy hands in fields
of metal fowl whose dipping necks and dripping beaks
pluck slimy wet black worms with tails that have

no end out of the earth. Iyiniwok are spurned
as deadbeats, good to fit-up with a well-placed boot,
who lean on beer-pissed walls, emaciated cattle not
worth rustling, strays best left to their fate
on wintry plains. Tribes pass this way like tides, the drip
of every journey scored, cell by painstaking cell,
in ivory bones, totems telling the payback gods "Come soon."
She sits beside three youth chewing on their bloodlines.
News from Kibish that one native placenta long
ago first bred our kind has yet to reach these parts. She sighs.
We're different from eagles, coyotes, hippopotami,
not from this fated sibling-hood, you there, me here,
one heart one blood. So better give it up and kiss
the rough cheeks of this old Assiniboine rose . . .

Blooming in Barcelona

Gaudi's Park Güell is what we dreamed
in our back yard scavenging from the dust
bowl midden near the fence under a dull
green ackee tree. We searched for broken bits
of pottery to use as hopscotch taws
indigo emerald cerulean blue
and now and then the burgundy of dried
blood or salt-pork-and-beans in big tureens
flung by deserted wives their lives
splintering with the porcelain to serve
the simple pleasures of small boys
and giddy girls discerning history
in Delft or rare translucent bits
of chinaware or rude fat colours splotched

to make bright foreign fruit! And Gaudi on
a bare hillside looking out on a sea
the dust as dry the sky as blue
doing just what we did. Create
a medium pour water on the dirt
and mush it into mud then shape a wall
a house a curvy tower with a cross
and stick the shining bits and pieces in.
Raise up a town with paths and avenues
of candy coloured cobblestones as Antoni
of Catalan not long before gathered
his midden scraps to make a park
of mythic beasts what we scrawled in
our book of dirt blooming in Barcelona.

Bluesman*

It have all kind: Pushkin, Dumas, and, him same one
say so, Vincent Van Gogh. Him tell him bro, Theo
to smoke a pipe, "Is a good tonic for de blues,
which take me over, dese days, now and den."
Him reason, "How you figure folks see me?
A ragamuffin... lowest of de low."
Him say, "Painters come like a family,
a mix-up mix-up bad for all o we
for everybody fighting the next one."
Him tell Christina, "No mind you's a whore
from where I sit, you irie, evermore."
Him recommend, "Don't yield before the end . . . "
Blowing him mind with a wild brush like Miles.
Like Don painting the scene with him trombone.

*Van Gogh's words are slightly adapted from his letters in
Vincent by Himself ed. Bruce Bernard (London: Time Warner), 2004.

Trois hommes: un rêve

You had a thing with Geraldine but we two shot across
the parkway anyway (you let me borrow you)
to safety on the Hudson's bank. "Rive droit,"
you said, "safe for a convent girl lost in
New York. La Grande Pomme est une Salomé!"
you kissed my nose, "saucy putain she veils
her sagging bits in smog, working backhand
past Harlem past George Washington's
suspension bridge. Don't its smudged U look like
a hammock in the steam?" Drunk with the day,
my love-on-loan, the sun, I stride beside
this arrogant Kwéyol cock-bottom man,
smiling Anansi with a sweet invite. "Let me
tickle your belly button—from inside."

I never knew when you, Louis and Jacques
set off to free Haiti. We'd meet again
when my son reading *Papa Doc* called out
your names, three guys who didn't live to man-
age mortgages, see your kids grow, coach ball,
get a rum belly, dance merengue with
a graying love (so open, close, glissant, what hips,
what toes), sit outside in cafés on Old Broadway,
whistle the women with the proudest stride
in the New World, see Michaëlle Jean become
head of this northern home on native land;

fellows who didn't live to see the last
millennium, your proudly severed heads
displayed on poles by the Tonton Macoutes.

I wish for you three on that day of wrath,
that dies irae when your blood ran hot
into the dusty Haitian dirt, that day
New York, blinking its harlot's eye,
trolled yet another john, I wish hills blue
with mist, green with the vegetation strife
has slashed and burned in your republic. I wish
a knife that's whisper edged, a blade that slides
across your throats clean as the peasant cut
by Guinea grass as he finds feed for goats
early before day dawns, a coup for love
past struggle, past the bright exit of blood
that cedes your freedom as you lose
your heads to that sweet dream of Haiti.

Poor Execution

They're scars carved on my soul, these friends
with heads chopped off, Richard, Julie,
Richard named like my bro not long before
shot through his gut. "So who want to go first?"
A small man with a knife extravagant
enquires. Its camber edge repeats a smile
a goodly devil's benefit. Forty years since
you'd slipped a chain around my neck. See here.
Photos. I have them still. "Surprise!" breathed from
that Buddha face, those eyes mild mouths under
the black moustaches of your brows. Mary's
medallion on a thread of gold, your gift caught at
my throat. Was Miss Lady, your housekeeper, the one
whose son would slit yours, that Madonna of New Day

bearing her jug, golden ortanique flame,
a glow extraordinaire, a spill of brilliance
sweet and sour like the pork that Jimmy Chen
and you concocted as you laughed at Dawn
and me wondering how you cooked so well,
so fast? She poured us glasses with a smile
that chaffed the long verandah at first light,
day glinting cool as a stone sharpened knife,
day gleaming bright as red beads on the grass,
a woman with the sun inside her mouth,
a woman with a son inside her skin,

a woman with your death in the slight bump
of belly underneath her apron's white,
clenched fist only just threatening.

Did they make you watch Julie's screams purple
as she blew out her life with every breath
she drew to keep it in? Or was it that
as you begged to go last, hoping to hold
her as they sliced a smile into her throat,
he strummed his pick across your sanxian neck
and crimson burbled your reply under
your chin? Soft ever, how did you deserve
this reckoning? Not that it matters since
you are all dead: Julie, Dickie, Brian, Burt,
Richard, Carlington, Faith, Hope . . . Call the roll
of thousands and there is no lesson we
can learn but that we did not do for our fellows all
we needed to. And we will keep on dying till we do.
.

One Time Jamboree—Darfur, Maybe?

Ku ya! No one celestial jamboree!
One place where sense and spirit can agree,
a corner whole night rattling calabash,
whirling, twirling, billowing cumuli
of skirts make to catch pickni any time
them little knee give out! But busha take
him staff, crook with a Janus head, a two-
way tongue, and slay them stroke by stroke. Is him
take bomb erase this marketplace where street
meet street, make it so poor we girls, houses
on fire, fields trod to dust, force flat down on
we back, we two legs bruck apart by dogs
with pestilential pricks that write death on
we womb as them condemn corpse after little corpse.

We carry them, no mind them bound
to dead, no mind we bound to dead. Expel
them like goat shit. Black dots with lecherous lips
that suck on empty dugs speckle this piazza where
we use one time to spread peanut, pumpkin,
pineapple, cocoa, corn. Ku bwana how
him set him sight straight past we labour pangs,
birth-water, navel-string, placenta, blood,
caul, trimmings that the old ones scrape
up deep at night and steal away to hide
underneath any stump them call a tree.

Come morning time, cock crow but green still in
these fields under tight lock and key until
rain break it free. So who going rally clouds?

Employ covert intelligence to track
the buds of sweat that bloom at day clean on
this grass? Marshal a force to dribble down
and damp the earth? Who going embed new posts
for huts? Run ploughs to ground? Shoot seeds
into the soil? Engage in combat hand-
to-hand with pests? Was a time once when pickni lap
around we ankles like warm morning waves
splashing in trash, leaves, old newspaper, as
them creep like neap tide up we foot. When we going put
we hand akimbo, sway we hip, beat exultation on
these drums again? When heels going tattoo thanks
in this soil's skin? Which priest going purge the curse
upon this place, give we back joy, restore we to we kin?

Remembering Nothing

For Kamau Brathwaite

Minnesota: Dakota, for water stained with sky. There is
a continuing candlelight vigil for peace on a bridge across
the Mississippi in Minnesota, once a week, every week.

Let me remember nothing, not recall
this watchful bridge of fireflies that spans
a torrent with a name we schoolers spelled,
a pride of little cats unfettered from
the cages of our elementary zoo, who screeched
"M-I, crooked letter crooked letter I, crooked
letter crooked letter I, hunch back hunch
back I – that's how you spell Mi/ssi/ssi/ppi!"
The vigil fires watch one night every week,
week after week a humming loop of light,
bright chant against the Babylon of war.
Dakota people join the elements
to make a name for water stained with sky.
So Minnesota writes its liquid prayer.

Let me forget the brethren and their queens,
jacketed men and their fat bougie wives,
students war torn from skirmishes inside
the muddy trenches of the minibus,
beggars, vendors, workers in the health trade,
the tourist trade, the education trade,

the trades of politics and government,
joined with sweat-pasted fingers to declare
before the Mighty Eagle's embassy:
"You people better stop this war." These tilt
the forces: Arab men tortured in Abu Ghraib,
Sioux warriors cut off at Wounded Knee,
Darfurian women firked, numberless slaves
wave after wave corralled in this green sea.

Let me not recollect you ached to fight,
sharpies manoeuvring death contrivances
who conned the credulous with WMDs
to raise crusades against the infidel—
and there are those who don't believe in hell?
Those silver pieces changing, changing hands
for guns, grenades, tanks, rockets, missiles, bombs,
the miscellaneous tambourines of bone-rattling war.
All you with palms crossed by those pretty coins?
Beware the anthem rising in your throats.
Beware your fingers plucking at those strings.
Beware your feet tap-tapping to the notes.
What if the show you staged and took to play
abroad, is revived on the Great White Way?

Bill Belfast and Lizzie Bell
In part a found poem

Efcaped on Thurfday evening, the eighteenth
instant a Negro Servant, property
of Michael Wallace the subfcriber, here below,
his name Belfast although known commonly
as Bill. At time of the elopement he was in
the fervice of William Forfyth, Esquire,
and had attempted twice to board a ship
which lay in harbour, bound to Newfoundland,
but was thwarted. Likely he may endeavour ftill
to make efcape that way. Therefore mafters
of coafters along fhore, or others bound to fea,
are hereby forewarned from taking him off
at their peril, for if found out they will
be profecuted, with the utmoft vigour of the law.

l am a stout-made fellow, six feet high,
of a mild temper and good countenance,
my black skin smooth, unmarked by disease,
my mouth with full complement of sound teeth,
born in South Carolina twenty-seven years
ago, fled from enslavement there as a
ship's hand, veteran sailor until caught
again and brought to work in Halifax.
l own the cloaths upon my back: an old
short coat, elbows worn out; duffil trowsers,

much worn; round hat, old black silk handkerchief.
Resident in this Province for ten years, I speak
softly and well, being the mark of one who is his own
person, for I am such, determined as I am to liberty.

The wind urges a night as slow as mud.
I wait amid barrels of salted cod
for Lizzie Bell, slave like me, let as laundress to
soldiers in barracks on Grottingen Street. 'Tis her
talent as healer, coupled with my own
as carpenter and cook has gained us berth
on the *Creole,* boat bound for London town
at the next tide, a risk I have made worth
the captain's while, for just now Lizzie brings
our few things and a wallet with savings
put by these past ten years. It buys from him pretense
we are at liberty. Listen! I hear her steps and see
in the half-light, her form. What's this? Company?
Oh Lizzie? Lizzie! You've not betrayed me?

Spoiled our chance of freedom? A shout: "Stop her!"
chased by my own, "Run Lizzie! Quick! This way!"
"You there—seize the black wench! And you! After
that wretch! With luck he's chattel that will pay
a goodly price as well!" Lizzie is light
as mist, smart as the slice of Massa Forsyth's whip.
Our bags she's tied about her, in her hands
my purse and a rush torch she hurls at them.
But woe! She trips, slips, falls, fights to her feet,

head down, fingers fumbling, then turns and throws.
Soldiers scramble for gold amidst the cobblestones.
Aboard, she weeps. "I threw them all you'd saved!"
I pat my breast and smile. "Nigger head long!" Lizzie hugs me.
"Now we are good as any man!" We hurry up the sea.

Thomas Thistlewood and Tom

Shit in my mouth. He makes my woman put
her bottom in my face and push her doo-
doo in between my lips. When she stops he
says, "More! You black bitch, more! Shove it out till
it bung a clog inside his throat or I
will strip your back until it makes
a bleeding pair with his." I watch her ass:
shit flecks clung to the petals in that tight
chrysanthemum come to my mouth again.
I tell myself: "So many days I dig the soft
ground of her front, water it, plant my seed.
watch it breed in her belly. If one day
I have to eat the stinking fruit it voids to live,
see my mouth here. Come. Fill it with her excrement."

My name is Tom. It is this fiend's as well.
He is no person, nor no man, nor common visitor
from hell. When evil folded tight inside
its shell so that sky waters would not wash
it clean, and hid, and aged, fermenting, made
a beard, a mouth, and hands and feet and spleen,
the need to work woe on a human being,
it was hatching this snake. He sleeps
to dream the vilest cruelty and wakes
to undertake it. Devilry is his invention.
I cannot fight rapine and pillage, violence

past thought, hate simmered to its essence. I
can love even to eating my love's shit.
No yellowbelly demon unmans me. Watch me do it.

Great-Granny Mac

Before Mister Bellmartin buy Great-Gran
she work into the pickni gang on a
plantation that belong to Mr Serle,
a backra man. That white man own her family—
mother, two brother, two sister, and she.
"He was a cruel man," my Great-Gran say.
"He love a whip. The cat o' nine was like
a flask of wine to him. He could get drunk
with lashing slaves. When his arm hoist is like
you see inebriation rise inside
his veins, his muscles, brain, his whole entire flesh
on fire. He lash man, woman, pickni too.
Even his friends advise, 'Don't be a fool.
Why, man, you're spoiling your own property!

"'You paid good money for those blacks!'
He answer: 'So—I flog them as I please.'
One day Mr Serle take in sudden with
belly workings. When Doctor come he cannot find
no remedy. 'If I were you, I'd change
the cook,' he recommend. 'Some nigger trying
to poison me? I'll rid me of the lot of them.'
Backra break up our family. Sell us
all bout. I bawling watch my brothers go
two different ways. I see one bigger sis
leave for Green Island; the next one they send
to Annotto Bay. They haul my Ma over Diablo

to the far north shore. Me, smallest, stay
on a estate in town. Mr Bellmartin purchase me.

"The day I see him, little most I drop
down from the sight. Top hat and ruffles, riding crop,
barouche—this man as black as night! When he
buy me, I was seven years old. For days
I suffer fever in my head. Don't rise, don't eat,
don't sleep. Make up my mind to dead. Then Ma
come in a dream and say, 'Madeleine, best you let go of us.
Put us away inside.' I do as Ma say. Rise
next day. I still can hear her whispering,
'Madeleine.' At Bellmartin's I turn cunning.
More times they catching me with book, paper
and pen. I know if they find any slave
with them things was a big-time crime. But chile,
my navel string cut on deceit, dissembly, lie.

"Tricky like Brer Anansi I maintain,
lip quivering, 'I only have such things
because Miss Meggie cannot bear to play
with any foolish darky girl.' Meggie
is black as me but my excuse don't fall
askew on any ear. I go on with
my tale. 'She say that I best learn to read
and write—and cipher too. I try
my best, sir, though it's hard. I always likes
to oblige.' Dropping a curtsy, I open
my big eyes bold, make four with his. And I

make sure I learn to read like a machine.
Poor Meggie she struggle with words dark like
her own black skin. I eat those words like they is food.

"Time I become fourteen I cipher well
enough to help keep books for the estate.
'This is my smartest nigger.' So declare
Bellmartin and he rent me out to some
small-holding folks who are too poor themselves
to maintain help full time to render their
accounts. I never like it from the first.
I know one of them small-hold man was going
grab hold of me and take his dim-wit purple pen
and write his seed inside my abdomen.
And when it happen, Jesus know I curse
Bellmartin and his friend. It leave me just
one course. When I learn numbers I make sure
to study doctor too—I know plenty

"from doctresses inside slave barracks and
I con from backra healing book. So I
know what to do to make ill well and the
reverse—to make well ill. I work my spell
and make Bellmartin sick. He lie there black
skin turning grey, hair dropping out.
No morsel pass his mouth that stay inside
his gorge. No spoon of drink slide easy down
his throat. When he get thin like gruel, his skin
like ashes, lips crack-up white like old paper, I

approach one night: 'Mr Bellmartin, sir,
Is me. Madeleine. Sir, I could boil a bush
I find, see if it help you.' A faint light
brighten his eye dishwater dull inside

"his shriveled head. 'But sir, if it fail and
you die, I need for you to write
a notice saying it was not my medicine
kill you. And sir, if you get well I need
a paper saying I, Madeleine Lazare
Mungo, am free.'" Great-Granny Mac tell me
it was a black slave-owning man that set
her and her belly free after he own
her for thirteen long years. From I was small
my Great-Gran was forever telling some
dramatic tale, and me, poor me, easy to fool,
take them as gospel truth. The rest indulge
her, "Great-Granny, for sure you can spin yarns
better than Brer Anansi self." She suck her teeth, tell me,

"Don't mind the lot of them. I put you in
the will." When she was ninety-nine my Great-
Gran died. At her graveside, wispy, spectral,
was a stranger nearly as old as Granny Mac
and lighter skin, but her dead stamp. "Please ma'am, are you
any relation to our beloved deceased?"
This from Jeffroy, Gran's eldest son, a courtly white-
haired gentleman bidding guests welcome at
the wake. A long suck-teeth just like Great-Gran's.

"How any man could old like you, Jeffroy,
and stupid so? Look hard into my face.
I bear Ma's name, Madeleine. I am the first-born one.
That time she get way from Bellmartin's place—
is me was in her belly when she run!"

Litany on the Line

Bad news again on the long distance line:
a growth flourishing in my sister's throat.
I think if one can spill hot coffee on oneself
and sue the restaurant and win, perhaps
a legal eagle with a well-tuned bill
could whistle up a case against AT&T
and Mama Bell. Two years ago on this
same phone, Lizzie told me and Mary Joan
that they'd shot Richard dead.
Across the trans-Atlantic line I hear
the ocean sizzle where infected earth
burning with fever oozes pus along a rupture in
its crust. I see the flickering photospores
inside the eyes of deep-sea fish. I hear

the cries of jettisoned black men,
women and children, not yet slaves, just worth
less than insurers paid for cargo spoiled en route.
Slitting this Carib basin's diamond skin
they flung its glints aside and burrowed in.
A person dies. It changes everything.
They died. No alteration? Nothing changed?
Except forever afterwards ships, boats
and planes with trained, skilled crews
and honed and hardened pilots fell
into that grave triangle for the Human Trade.

And flying now above the blue Bermudas, look
and you will see, along a coral ridge of white,
dark looping t's, like long canoes, like open crypts.

O, lay the ancestors to rest inside
these cursive curls with litanies.
Anoint their necks, their ankles, wrists,
with sacred oil. Put wampum shells upon
their eyes and set bouquets of trembling
anemones between their fingers and their toes.
Sing sankeys, beat the drums to dredge
up greed, harpoon it like Leviathan
and beach it where the carrion birds will pick
its pink meat from its bones. Blessed are you
buried in this blue dirt. Blessed are you
who never reached this side. Blessed are you
who listen as the tribe burbles its grievous news
across these fibre-optic threads. Blessed are you.

Who Loves Not Self, Loves Not

For Joe McHugh S J

If Robert Southwell made a hymn for a soulful boy child
'whose heart no thought, whose tongue no word, whose hand
no deed defiled;' if Hopkins sprung new rhythms for
his falcon spry on wing, wind hovering bird,
up full, fiercely flaming on Spirit's swing, is it not Lord
that these are saints who have selves that they love,
and loving self so, and so loved by self, can others love?
You Self have said that we must love others
as we love self. But what if we despise
that craft, sweet purling that your Father set
about as he wove every self each in
his mother's womb? What if inside us, animus
flares furious, eating all air, prayer? What then, most valorous
when we say no to God's grandeur in us?

Wade in the Water

She set down hat and cane on the bank side,
writer shape-shifting into river maid,
pockets inlaid with stones, storyteller's
ballast to steady her on course. Same so
our Grandpa Sam took to the salt of this soft sea,
shirt bright as the new sun, clean as the day's,
amber face sad as our Jamaican owl's.
"Run, Roy! Run! Boysie! Get the priest!" Poor Gran.
She never got it was a doctor man
they should have fetched. Now Mama decades on,
wading in waters that she didn't choose,
negotiates the narrows of her bed
and follows Gramps as cancer rapids spread
into her lungs and unto liquidation sweep her off.

One time she'd dally with the deep, Sundays or mid-
week afternoons when we careened into
the Harbour's weedy warmth, eyes pasted to
her back. She'd panic us, throats, hearts, bellies
tied to her sneaky strides, her dithering.
Dive or no dive? Same so our captive great-
great-great-grandma Mungo tottered on deck,
unshackled for the dance, sized up the rail.
Jump or no jump? The body snatchers tripped
her up as she shambled to gain the purchase of the side.
Great-great-grandfather Nirmal crossed another way,

the kala pani nursing at the breast,
suckling its dark into his DNA.
It was his element. He thrived in it.

For him black waters were the muddy wake
behind the hurricane, storms' afterbirth
roiling in gullies gobbed with rotting leaves
and carcasses, a wash herding men, carts,
beasts, cargo, carriages to sea, harvest
for his quick eye and lissome limb that yielded wheels,
knives, clothes, paraphernalia for the poor.
Black waters were sloshing night soil in leaky pails,
rich brew that jealous Africans indicted for
fat coolie cabbages, gorgeous spinach.
"Shit vegetables! Wee-wee callaloo!"
His waterfalls were winds that tongued compliant fields
of cane in Krishna's bubble sky, brides sailing in
red saris at days' end, saffron ripples of sun.

Nights I can't sleep I call up ghosts: rose from the Ouse,
a bone-white mermaid pipes a slippery tune,
hat on her head, fist firm around the reed
with which she inscribes melodies.
Great-great-grandfather Nirmal rises up full fathom five,
arm over arm slices the sea of heaven with bold strokes
to buoy up Mama as she slips beyond the flat
world's edge, surfacing with her on his fins.
Great-great-grandma Mungo dynasties soughed
out of her stolen gut unfolds magnificent pinions.

Summoned they lift in flight, salt drops flashed off
impatient from great umber wings, souls in
a flock of homing seraphim who sing
praises, lips wetted for glory everlasting.

Yarn Spinner

Inside she sits and spins, decanting gold
and silver from her wrists. Her fingers bleed.
Day, and then night. Myriad windows perch
above her head, brilliant birds. Through them
she cannot see the river pirouette
from a valley hung high, tumble, kneel deep
into a basin blue as chiming bells set in
obsidian rocks. Night, and then day, but she
cannot observe the stars, the sun. She scoffs air,
laps sweat off her chin. Straining to listen, finds
she cannot hear even the wind. The walls
leach marrow from her bones. The room
adjusts around her shrinking frame of mind.
She teases out a winking thread, curls it

about a spool, then wheels and comes again.
Rich filaments bite through her skin as she
construes the pile of unspun wool, rovings
of thought, symbols of winding cord, strings she
makes hum, imagine up a poem to twist
the tongue, cable to match a letter to
a sound, a drill that interweaves syntax
of word and necessary word, a song
to bring a measured meter to the hands
that drum on ancient wood. But this can't be a life.
Flapping flamboyant wings the windows preen

and squawk, a flock cruising landscapes she will
not see again. The river in the sun
spits, spurts, explodes resplendent as a veil

let fall to hide a bride. Marry she won't
locked in this tower where time goes. Her green
skin crawls, fluted as wrinkled sea. Once she
was brown and curious in the world. Now her
illumination is a crusted bulb
on a high wire. How did she come to this,
within without an inkling of out, intent
on weaving meaning as she strips it from
herself? And still she feeds the iridescent mound
so thick and plentiful it steals the light.
And are you sad alone? Not when I spin.
And are you sorry for the yarns you make?
No, for they keep the children warm. What if
you die spinning a thread? Die, yes, but never dead . . .

Acknowledgements

To the Ontario Arts Council (Works in Progress and Writers' Reserve programs) and the Toronto Arts Council, both of which supported the writing of this book, and to the 2009 jury of the Canada Council Literary Awards, who highly recommended it for funding.

To Martin especially, for his many readings and re-readings of the poems, and to the profs from Arizona, for keeping me going; to the online writing group and to my fellow poets, mentors, friends and family, who are too many to name, for reading all or part of the manuscript at various times, and for other practical help, encouragement and good counsel; to Rethabile Masilo and Geoffrey Philp, for providing internet spaces that celebrate poetry; to my agent, Margaret Hart, for finding the manuscript a home, and to Nurjehan Aziz and M G Vassanji for welcoming it at TSAR.

"Family Story, Only Child's Version" is a reworking of a shorter poem which first appeared in *Journey Poem* (Sandberry Press, 1989). A somewhat different "Great-Granny Mac" appeared in *The True Blue of Islands* (Sandberry Press, 2005). Other poems were first published in the anthology, *Jubilation!* edited by Kwame Dawes (Peepal Tree Press, 2012) and in the journals, *BIM Arts for the 21st Century, Callaloo, Canopic Jar, Caribbean Quarterly, Caribbean Review of Books* (online), *Jamaica*

Journal and *The Literary Review of Canada.* "Temitope" is forthcoming in the anthology, *The Great Black North: Poetry by African Canadians,* to be published by Frontenac Press in spring 2013. "Counting the Ways and Marrying True Minds," "Jamboree: Darfur, maybe?" and "Yarn Spinner" first appeared on Geoffrey Philp's blogspot; "Zambesi Paen 1995" appeared on Rethabile Masilo's blog, Poéfrika, and "Who Loves Not Self" on my blog, Jahworld.

"Litany on the Line," "Trois hommes, un rêve" and an early version of "Reading at 4:00 am," combined as one poem, was shortlisted for the CBC Literary Awards in 2007. "Blooming in Barcelona" was shortlisted for The Bridport Prize (UK) in 2008.